THE **100+** SERIES™

Reproducible Activities

Daily Warmups

Math Problems & Puzzles

Grade 2

Published by Instructional Fair • TS Denison
an imprint of

McGraw Hill **Children's Publishing**

Editors: Linda Triemstra, Sara Bierling

 **Children's Publishing**

Published by Instructional Fair • TS Denison
An imprint of McGraw-Hill Children's Publishing
Copyright © 2003 McGraw-Hill Children's Publishing

Send all inquiries to:
McGraw-Hill Children's Publishing
3195 Wilson Drive NW
Grand Rapids, Michigan 49544

Daily Warmups: Math Problems & Puzzles—grade 2
ISBN: 0-7424-1792-1

1 2 3 4 5 6 7 8 9 PHXBK 08 07 06 05 04 03

Table of Contents

NCTM Standard	Problem Number
Number and Operations	4, 8, 9, 11, 15, 17, 18, 21, 24, 25, 27, 30, 31, 33, 34, 35, 36, 42, 43, 44, 45, 47, 51, 53, 54, 55, 58, 61, 66, 67, 68, 72, 74, 75, 79, 83, 88, 89, 90, 92, 103, 107, 112, 113, 117, 122, 123, 126, 130, 135, 150, 158, 162, 163, 168, 171, 173, 176, 177, 178, 180, 181, 185, 188, 192, 194, 196, 200, 201, 205, 210, 212, 217, 219, 220, 224, 225, 227, 229, 233, 234
Algebra	6, 7, 13, 20, 22, 26, 29, 37, 40, 46, 62, 63, 70, 73, 76, 81, 93, 95, 97, 104, 105, 108, 110, 111, 115, 118, 119, 121, 124, 125, 129, 132, 138, 139, 145, 155, 156, 157, 166, 167, 169, 170, 182, 183, 189, 198, 202, 207, 211, 213, 223, 226, 230, 232
Geometry	2, 10, 23, 32, 41, 52, 60, 85, 96, 98, 106, 114, 127, 134, 137, 143, 147, 151, 154, 164, 174, 184, 228
Measurement	1, 3, 14, 19, 28, 38, 57, 64, 71, 80, 82, 84, 99, 102, 109, 128, 131, 136, 140, 141, 144, 146, 149, 153, 159, 161, 172, 190, 191, 193, 195, 199, 204, 206, 209, 215, 221, 231
Data Analysis and Probability	12, 48, 59, 69, 78, 87, 101, 120, 148, 152, 165, 179, 197, 218, 222
Problem Solving	5, 16, 39, 49, 50, 56, 65, 77, 86, 91, 94, 100, 116, 133, 142, 160, 175, 186, 187, 203, 208, 214, 216

Introduction

This book is one in a series of books from kindergarten through grade 8. Each book provides a wide variety of challenging and engaging grade-appropriate problems and puzzles from all areas of the math curriculum. Each book contains 234 problems and puzzles, one for each day of the school year plus more. All are keyed to the appropriate NCTM standards, and many are designed for hands-on problem solving using common classroom manipulatives. Several problems call for the use of tangrams. For your convenience, we have included a reproducible set on page 5. Other problems call for protractors, dice, pentominoes, and calculators. However, most problems require only paper and pencil and a little brainpower.

Each page contains two problems or puzzles. The problems are reproducible and are suitable for overhead use. Most offer ample space for problem solving. The problems and puzzles in this book are designed to be solved within 15 minutes, but most will take 5 minutes or less. These problems are great for use as early-morning warm-ups or for the beginning of math class and can be worked independently or in groups. You can also assign problems as homework or as a math lab activity. Another idea is to use these problems in class competitions. Which group or individual will be the first to solve the problem?

Work through a few problems with your students before they begin to work independently or in a group. As you do so, it's important to model a problem-solving process. Stress that many problems have multiple solutions. Then, watch as your students grow and develop their own problem-solving strategies and gain a new appreciation for math.

Tangrams

Measurement

Show the time two ways.

What time do you get up on school mornings?

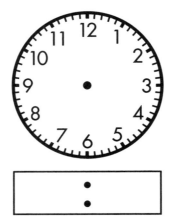

Geometry

Using tangrams, match the shapes.

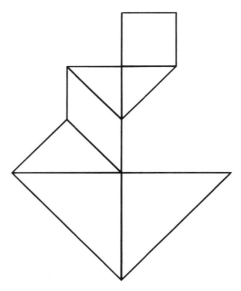

Measurement

3

If it is 5 A.M., what time was it 8 hours ago?

If it is 5 A.M., how many hours will it be until 12 noon?

What time will it be 8 hours after 5 A.M.?

Number and Operations

4

André found 15 ladybugs. He then found 14 more ladybugs. How many ladybugs were there in all?

Problem Solving

Use the clues to find the number.

Clue 1 The number is an even number.

Clue 2 The number is the sum of doubles.

Clue 3 The number is greater than 16.

Clue 4 The number is less than 20.

Algebra

Cross out the thing in each row that does not belong.

Algebra

Use the rule to find the numbers in the OUT row.

Rule: Add 2

IN	4	5	6	7	8
OUT	6	7			

Number and Operations

What fraction is shaded?

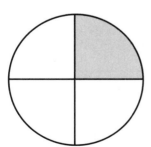   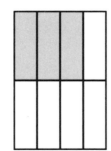   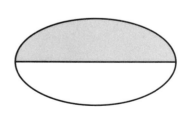

Number and Operations

Solve each problem.

$74 + 15 =$

$52 - 10 =$

$76 - 28 =$

$83 + 38 =$

Geometry

Use cubes to make the shapes. Look for a pattern. Make a fourth shape. Follow the pattern.

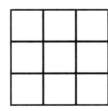

first   second   third

Number and Operations

There are 20 oranges. Each costs $0.05. Estimate how much all of the oranges would cost. Then find the actual cost.

Data Analysis and Probability

Maria puts 4 green cubes, 2 red cubes, and 1 yellow cube into a bag. She shakes the bag. Then she closes her eyes and pulls out 1 cube. What color cube will she probably pull out of the bag?

Algebra

Look for a pattern in each group of numbers. Write the number that comes next.

4, 7, 10, 13, 16, _____

20, 16, 12, 8, 4, _____

Measurement

Latoya ate breakfast at 7:00 A.M. She took 15 minutes to finish eating. What time did Latoya finish eating breakfast?

Draw the hands on the clock.

Number and Operations

15

A baby elephant weighs 92 pounds. A baby shark weighs 26 pounds. How many pounds do the shark and the elephant weigh in all?

Problem Solving

16

Apples are cheaper than peaches. Nectarines cost more than peaches. Which fruit is the most expensive? Which fruit is the least expensive?

Number and Operations

Joaquin has 1 nickel, 1 quarter, and 2 pennies. What is the total value of the coins he has?

Number and Operations

Use <, >, or = to compare each set of numbers.

165   156

465   459

265   344

Measurement

19

Use linking cubes.

Estimate how many cubes you think it would take to measure each object. Then measure each object with your cubes. What is the difference between your estimate and the actual measurement?

the length of a book

the width of your desk

Algebra

20

Use the rule to find the numbers that complete the OUT row.

Rule: Add 4

IN	6	8	10	12	14
OUT	10	12			

Number and Operations

Each class at Crestview School is working to raise $100.00 for the library. Akiko's class raised $25.00, then $2.00, $20.00, $7.00, $30.00, and $20.00. Estimate whether Akiko's class has raised $100.00. Now figure the actual amount of money that her class has raised. If the class doesn't have enough money, how much more money do they need to raise?

Algebra

Cross out the thing in each row that does not belong.

Geometry

There are 5 children lined up for ice cream. Ryan is first in line. Emily is between Mei and Hector. Imani is not next to Ryan. Where is each child in the line?

Number and Operations

If pieces of fudge are $0.30 each, how much fudge can you buy for $2.00? How much change will you receive?

Number and Operations

Aleesha has 1 nickel, 1 quarter, 1 dime, and 1 penny. What is the total value of the coins she has?

Algebra

Fill in the missing numbers to show equal values. Complete each equation.

3 + 3 = 2 + _____

_____ + 4 = 5 + 3

_____ + 5 = 6 + 4

6 + 6 = _____ + 2

Number and Operations

Sergei orders a burger for $3.75, a soda for $0.75, and a sundae for $1.95. How much does he spend in all?

Sergei pays for his food with a $10.00 bill. How much change does he receive?

Measurement

The world's smallest frog, the Cuban frog, is less than $\frac{1}{2}$ inch long. About how long is this in centimeters?

Algebra

Connect the dots in each row to continue the pattern.

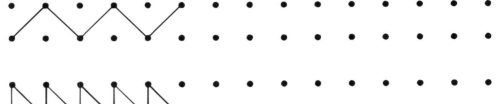

Number and Operations

Jamal bought a hamburger for $3.00. He had a half-off coupon. How much will the hamburger cost?

Number and Operations

What do 2 quarters and 5 dimes equal?

Geometry

Connect the dots to make each shape that is described.

Make a square.   Make a rectangle.   Make a triangle.

•   •   •   •   •   •   •   •   •

•   •   •   •   •   •   •   •   •

33 Number and Operations

What is the value of each set of flats, rods, and units?

_____ hundreds   _____ tens   _____ ones

_____ total

_____ hundreds   _____ tens   _____ ones

_____ total

34 Number and Operations

How many marbles in all are there?

If 3 friends share the marbles equally, how many marbles would each person get?

Number and Operations

Add.

25 + 27 =

18 + 36 =

49 + 15 =

73 + 14 =

Number and Operations

Subtract.

59 − 22 =

82 − 45 =

27 − 18 =

63 − 26 =

Algebra

Celinda is collecting crayons every day this week. On Monday she collected 2 crayons. On Tuesday she collected 4 crayons. On Wednesday she collected 8 crayons.

If the pattern continues, how many crayons will Celinda collect on Thursday? (Hint: Use a T-chart to record the pattern and solve the puzzle.)

Measurement

Write the value of the coins shown. Then write **<**, **>**, or **=** to show which group of coins has the larger value.

Problem Solving

Jessica and Tania are working on problem-solving statements. The one they are working on says, "Draw more flowers than birds." Jessica is drawing 3 flowers and 2 birds. Tania is drawing 6 flowers and 3 birds.

Draw another solution for the statement about flowers and birds.

Algebra

Look at the objects shown below. Think about how they are alike. Then think of three other objects that would be like them.

Geometry

Each shape shown below can be found in the rectangles. Shade in each shape in the rectangles.

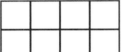  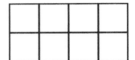 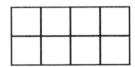

Number and Operations

Add.

251 + 148 =

594 + 302 =

135 + 211 =

813 + 165 =

Number and Operations

Write the number of coins it would take to equal a quarter.

_____ dimes + _____ nickels

or

_____ nickels

Number and Operations

Subtract.

657 – 326 =

874 – 521 =

986 – 724 =

598 – 320 =

Number and Operations

Sarah, Aliyah, and Miata collect stickers. Sarah has 12, Aliyah has 14, and Miata has 10. The girls want to combine their stickers and then divide them equally. How many stickers will each girl have?

Algebra

Find the pattern. Then draw what comes next.

□ △ □ △ □ △ □ _____

∩ // ∩ // ∩ // ∩ // _____

0-7424-1792-1 *Daily Warmups*

Number and Operations

A baby shark weighs 26 pounds. A baby hippo weighs 83 pounds. How much do they weigh in all?

Data Analysis and Probability

Tia has 12 round red beads and 3 square yellow beads in a bag. If Tia reaches into the bag and pulls out a bead, which shape bead do you think it will be? Why?

Problem Solving

Use counters.

There are 14 counters in a row. The counters are purple, blue, red, and orange. The first 5 counters are purple. The next 3 counters are red. Then there are the same number of blue and orange counters next to each other in line. How many blue counters are there?

Problem Solving

Ms. Organic planted 35 rows of tomato plants and 57 rows of green beans. It took her four days to do the planting. How many rows of beans and tomatoes did Ms. Organic have in all?

Number and Operations

Count in order. Fill in the missing numbers.

_____ _____ _____ 120

167 _____ _____ _____

_____ 150 _____ _____

_____ _____ 131 _____

Geometry

Use tangrams.

Use two or more tangram pieces to make a triangle. Find two different ways to make a triangle. Draw your answers.

Number and Operations

Use **<**, **>**, or **=**.

156   165

182   149

193   139

Number and Operations

Circle each group of coins that has a value of $0.10.

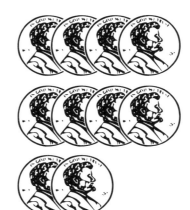

Number and Operations

Write the fractions for the black portion of each figure.

_____ black

_____ black

Problem Solving

Jumah has 6 coins in his pocket. The value of the coins is $0.51. What are the 6 coins?

57 Measurement

Measure each item using a centimeter ruler.

 _____ cm

 _____ cm

 _____ cm

58 Number and Operations

Compare. Use **<**, **>**, or **=**.

$4 + 2$ $12 - 6$

$6 + 6$ $3 + 9$

$9 - 2$ $2 + 5$

$2 + 6$ $18 - 9$

Data Analysis and Probability

Find the average of each group of numbers.

13, 12, 7, 3, 10

8, 12, 7, 8, 5

Geometry

Each shape can be found in the rectangles below. Shade in each shape in the rectangle at the bottom of the page.

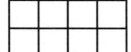 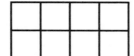 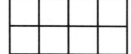

Number and Operations

Add or subtract.

239 + 119 =

946 − 217 =

184 + 185 =

716 − 518 =

Algebra

Shade in the first row to keep the pattern going.

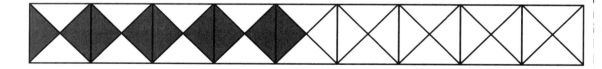

Now make your own pattern.

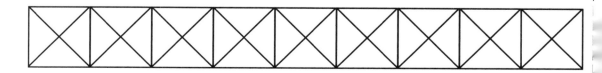

Algebra

Look at the numbers in the IN and OUT rows. Find the pattern between the IN and OUT numbers. Then use the pattern to fill in the missing numbers. Write the rule.

IN	0	1	2	3	4	5
OUT	3	4	5			

Measurement

Darius and Danica went on a hike with their family. They started at 8 A.M. They finished their hike after climbing over 6 hills. It took them 1 hour to climb over each hill. At what time did Darius and Danica finish their hike?

Problem Solving

Airline A has a fare of $412.00 to fly from Chicago to Los Angeles. The fare from Chicago to Boston is $335.00. How much more does it cost to fly to Los Angeles than to Boston?

Number and Operations

Write the fractions for the black portion of each figure.

_____ black   _____ black

Number and Operations

Use the clues to find the mystery number.

Clue 1 The number is between 0 and 3.

Clue 2 The number is closer to 3 than to 0.

Number and Operations

Use cubes.

Take 24 cubes. Put the cubes into 2 equal groups.

How many cubes are in each group? Draw your answer.

Put the cubes back together. Now put them into 3 equal groups.

How many cubes are in each group? Draw your answer.

Data Analysis and Probability

Survey the other students in your class: What is your favorite kind of fruit? Tally the results. Then draw a graph to show the data.

Algebra

Find each pattern. Then draw what comes next.

Measurement

Find ten things in your classroom that are less than 10 centimeters long. List them.

Number and Operations

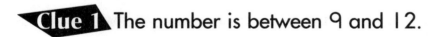

Use the clues to find the mystery number.

Clue 1 The number is between 9 and 12.

Clue 2 The number is closer to 12 than to 9.

Algebra

Find the pattern. Write what comes next.

3 3 2 3 3 2 3 3 2

Now draw or write you own pattern.

Number and Operations

Two different airlines schedule flights from Chicago to Atlanta at 11:45 A.M. and 3:45 P.M. If you miss the 11:45 A.M. flight, how long must you wait for the next flight?

Number and Operations

There are 5 boxes, each with 8 crayons in them. How many crayons are there in all? Draw a picture to show your answer.

Algebra

Use pattern blocks.

Match the shapes.

Draw the shape that comes next.

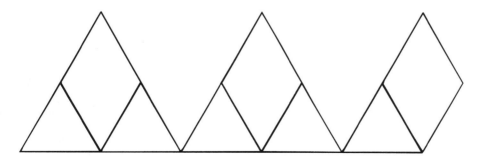

77 Problem Solving

Two farmers gave produce to a local food bank. Mr. Sunnyview gave away 14 bags of potatoes and 26 bags of carrots. Ms. Clearwater gave away 17 bags of potatoes and 25 bags of carrots. Who gave away more bags of produce? How many bags in all did both farmers give away?

78 Data Analysis and Probability

Find the average of the following numbers.

4, 6, 3, 7, 9, 1

17, 3, 6, 7, 2

Number and Operations

Write four number sentences that have an answer of 16. Write one with three addends.

Measurement

Find ten objects in your classroom that are more than 6 inches long. List them.

Algebra

Look at each number in the IN and OUT rows below.
Look for a pattern between the numbers.
Use the pattern to fill in the missing numbers.
Then write the rule.

IN	0	2	4	6	8	10
OUT	2	4	6			

Measurement

Amanda is going to the park with her family. They leave for Riverside Park at 9:00 A.M. They get to the park at 10:00 A.M. Amanda and her brother and sister help to carry the food to a table. Then they get out their ball and play until 10:30 A.M. For 1 hour and 30 minutes, they play on the swings and the slide. Then they have lunch.

Show at what time Amanda's family got to the park.

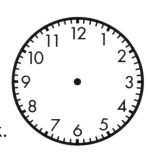

Show at what time Amanda's family ate lunch.

Number and Operations

Bryant and Antwon sorted books for the library's used book sale. On Monday they sorted 77 books. On Tuesday they sorted 44 fewer books than they did on Monday. On Wednesday they sorted 22 fewer books than they did on Tuesday. How many books did Bryant and Antwon sort altogether?

Measurement

Find ten objects in your classroom that are between 10 and 15 centimeters long. List them.

Geometry

Use tangrams.

Use this triangle as a unit of measurement.

How many units of area does each shape have?

_____ units of area   _____ units of area

Problem Solving

Anita goes to a yard sale with her mother. Anita has $1.32. She buys a stuffed bear for $0.85. How much money does she have left?

Data Analysis and Probability

Use cubes.

Put 1 red cube, 1 green cube, 1 yellow cube, and 1 blue cube into a paper bag. Shake the bag.

Take out 1 cube without looking. What color is it? Tally the result.

Put the cube back in the bag. Shake the bag.

Do this 16 times in all. Tally the result each time.

Did you get one color more often than the others? Did you get each color about the same number of times?

Did you have the same chance of getting each color?

Number and Operations

Write the fraction.

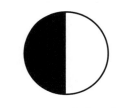

_____ black

_____ white

Number and Operations

Draw four ways to make $0.78.

Number and Operations

Write the value of the coins shown below.

Problem Solving

A gardener has 119 pots of daisies in his greenhouse. Each pot of daisies has 13 flowers blooming in it. How many blooming daisies are there in all?

Number and Operations

Add.

360 + 350 =

820 + 165 =

159 + 596 =

482 + 243 =

Algebra

Use pattern blocks.

Look for a pattern.

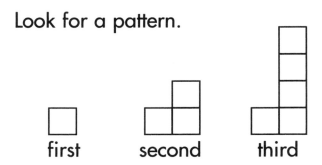

first   second   third

If the pattern continues in the same way, how many blocks will be in the fifth pattern?

Problem Solving

Sabrielle had $47.00. She earned $15.00 more by baby-sitting. Then she went to the mall with her parents and spent $19.00. How much money does Sabrielle have now?

Algebra

Color the squares to make the pattern AABBAABB.

A = blue   B = green

☐ ☐ ☐ ☐ ☐ ☐ ☐ ☐

Geometry

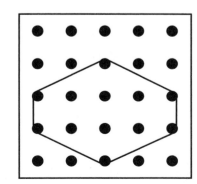

Use a geoboard.

Copy the shape on your geoboard.
Count the pins that the shape touches.

touches _____ pins

Algebra

Use blocks to build the shapes.
Look for a pattern.

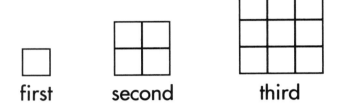

first   second   third

If the pattern continues in the same way, how many blocks will be in the fifth shape?

Geometry

Use a geoboard.

Copy the shape on your geoboard.
Count the sides. Count the corners.

_____ sides _____ corners

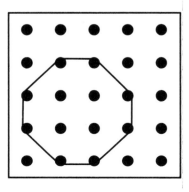

Measurement

Measure each item using an inch ruler.

Problem Solving

Chania has 7 coins in her pocket. Their value is $0.55. What are the coins?

101 Data Analysis and Probability

Look at the shoes of people in your classroom. Tally the kinds of shoes that people have: tie shoes, slip-on shoes, Velcro shoes, or some other kind of shoe. Make a graph to show the data.

102 Measurement

Use cubes.

Use the side of the cube as one unit of length.

Cover the shape shown below.

Count the number of units around the outside of the shape.

What is the perimeter of this shape? _____ units

Number and Operations

Write **<**, **>**, or **=** to compare the numbers.

8 + 5   6 + 9

4 + 9   6 + 8

14 − 7   16 − 9

17 − 8   4 + 7

Algebra

Put 5 blue cubes and 5 purple cubes in one side of a balance.

Put 7 red cubes and 3 orange cubes in the other side of a balance.

Write the equation.

_____ + _____ = _____ + _____

Algebra

Look for a pattern in the group of numbers. Then write the number that comes next.

7, 9, 12, 14, 17, _____

Geometry

Use tiles.

Look at the sheet of paper on your desk.

Estimate how many tiles it would take to cover the paper. Write your estimate: _____ tiles.

Now cover the piece of paper and count. Write your answer: _____ tiles.

Number and Operations

Alisha has between 15 and 20 crayons and markers in a box. There are 4 fewer crayons than markers. Draw the crayons and markers.

Algebra

Use pattern blocks to match the shapes. Look for a pattern. What comes next? Add blocks to show.

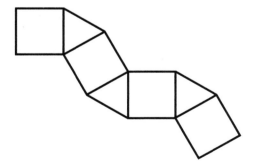

Now use blocks to make your own pattern.

Measurement

Find ten objects in your classroom that are between 10 and 15 inches long. List them.

Algebra

Fill in the missing numbers to show equal values.

7 + 7 = 8 + _____

_____ + 8 = 12 + 4

9 + _____ = 7 + 11

10 + 10 = _____ + 12

Algebra

Look at the pattern. Then write the next three letters.

A, C, E, G, I, _____, _____, _____

What is the pattern?

Number and Operations

Color

the second crayon yellow.
the fourth crayon blue.
the eighth crayon purple.
the fifth crayon orange.
the first crayon brown.
the third crayon red.
the seventh crayon black.
the sixth crayon green.

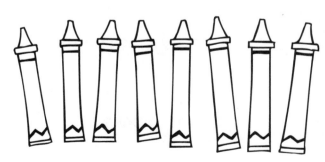

Number and Operations

Marta's family is going to the neighborhood art show. The show's organizers charge $4.00 for an adult to go to the show. The cost is half that amount for a child. There are 2 adults and 2 children in Marta's family. How much will it cost for everyone in her family to go to the art show?

Geometry

Use attribute blocks.

Jacob's younger brother, Joshua, has hidden three of Jacob's attribute blocks. The three blocks have these things in common:

The blocks are all different colors.
The blocks are all different shapes.
The blocks are all the same size.
The blocks are all the same thickness.

Which three attribute blocks could Joshua have taken?

Algebra

Use cubes and a balance.
Find the equal values.

Put 5 red cubes, 5 yellow cubes, and 5 orange cubes on one side of the balance.

Put 8 blue cubes, 2 green cubes, and 5 purple cubes on the other side of the balance.

Write the equation.

____ + ____ + ____ = ____ + ____ + ____

Problem Solving

Lianna and her mother are going to her school's bake sale. Pies are $6.00 each, including tax. If Lianna's mother has $25.00, how many pies can she buy?

Number and Operations

There were 22 second graders playing in a park. There were 10 students playing soccer. Another 4 students were playing tennis. Another group of 3 students were shooting baskets. The other students were resting. How many children were resting?

Algebra

Look at the pictures below. Write two things about how all of the pictures are alike. Then write two things about how all of the pictures are different.

Algebra

Look at the objects shown below.
Draw a circle around the things that you would find in your home. Draw a rectangle around the things that you would find outside. Draw a triangle around the things that you would find in your classroom.

Data Analysis and Probability

Find the average for each group of numbers.

9, 6, 7, 6

8, 3, 4, 3, 6, 0

Algebra

Use pattern blocks.

Look at the pattern blocks shown below.
Which ones do you think belong together? Why?

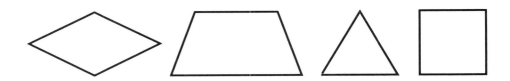

Number and Operations

Subtract.

$657 - 326 =$

$874 - 521 =$

$986 - 724 =$

$598 - 320 =$

0-7424-1792-1 *Daily Warmups*

Number and Operations

Two neighbors, Joe and Sam, have a friendly competition about their large gardens. Each man planted 12 rows of corn. It took Joe 12 days to plant his corn. Sam took only 9 days to plant corn. How many rows of corn were planted in all?

Algebra

Shade the boxes to keep the pattern going.

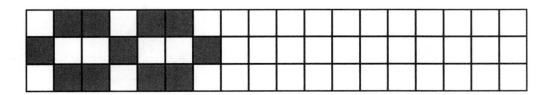

Algebra

Look at the pictures shown below.
Color the items you would find in your home blue.
Color the items you would find in your classroom red.
Color the items you would find outside green.

Number and Operations

Write the fraction for the black part of each figure.

_____ black   _____ black

Geometry

Count the sides on the presents. (Hint: Remember to count the sides that you can't see.)

Number of sides on all the presents _____

Measurement

Use a ruler to find each measurement.

How wide is the door of your classroom?

_____ inches   _____ centimeters

How long are your shoes?

_____ inches   _____ centimeters

How long is your pencil?

_____ inches   _____ centimeters

Algebra

Look at the numbers. Find the pattern. Then write the next three numbers.

15, 20, 25, 30, 35, _____, _____, _____

What is the pattern?

Make up your own number pattern.

Number and Operations

What is the value of each set of flats, rods, and units?

_____ hundreds _____ tens _____ ones

_____ total

_____ hundreds _____ tens _____ ones

_____ total

Measurement

Use **<**, **>**, or **=** to compare the amounts.

5 grams   5 kilograms

1,000 grams   1 kilogram

1 kilogram   900 grams

Algebra

Look at the sets of objects below.
List one way in which they are the same. Then list one
way in which they are different.

Problem Solving

Use the clues to find the mystery number.

Clue 1 The number is an odd number.

Clue 2 The number is less than 22.

Clue 3 The number is greater than 19.

Clue 4 The sum of the digits is 3.

Clue 5 The digit in the tens place is one more than the digit in the ones place.

Geometry

Use a geoboard.

Make the square. ☐

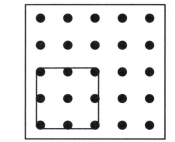

Then change the square to a triangle. Draw what you made. ◺

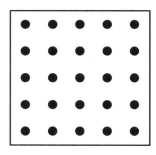

0-7424-1792-1 *Daily Warmups*

Number and Operations

Write the fractions.

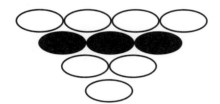
_____ black

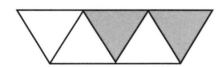
_____ white

Measurement

Read the questions. Make an estimate for each answer. Then find the actual total.

How many cars will drive past your school in three minutes? (Hint: Use a clock or stopwatch.)

Estimate _____   Measure _____

How many windows are in your school?

Estimate _____   Measure _____

Geometry

Look for cubes, cylinders, and spheres in your classroom. Make a list of them.

Algebra

Connect the dots in each row to keep the pattern going.

 0-7424-1792-1 *Daily Warmups*

Algebra

Look at the numbers in the IN and OUT rows below.
Look for a pattern between the IN and OUT numbers.
Use the pattern to fill in the missing numbers.

IN	0	1	2	3	4	5
OUT	5	6	7			

Write the rule.

Measurement

Fill a 1-liter measuring cup with water and look at it while you answer the questions below.

Will 5 liters of water fill a 5-gallon container?

Can you fill your bathroom sink with 1 liter of water?

Would 5 liters of water be better than 1 liter if you want to give your whole class a drink of water?

Measurement

Compare the weights given below. Circle the example in each pair that is lighter.

10 pounds   15 pounds

30 pounds   2 pounds

14 pounds   16 pounds

Problem Solving

Use the clues to find the mystery number.

Clue 1 The number is an even number.

Clue 2 The number is less than 8.

Clue 3 The number is greater than 5.

Clue 4 You say the number when you count by twos.

Clue 5 The number has one digit.

Geometry

Look at the shapes shown below.
Then think of other objects that are the same shape.
Draw the other objects. Write their names next to the
shapes below.

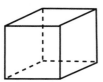 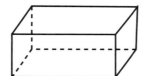

Measurement

Solve each problem.

21 centimeters + 4 centimeters =

12 centimeters + 13 centimeters =

17 centimeters + 3 centimeters =

Algebra

Floria is working in her flowerbeds. She made a chart to show how many flowers she planted each day. Look for a pattern.

How many plants will Floria plant on day 6?

Day	1	2	3	4	5	6
Number of Flowers	❋ ❋	❋ ❋ ❋ ❋	❋ ❋ ❋ ❋ ❋ ❋	❋ ❋ ❋ ❋ ❋ ❋ ❋ ❋	❋ ❋ ❋ ❋ ❋ ❋ ❋ ❋ ❋ ❋	

Measurement

Compare the weights shown below. Circle the example in each pair that is the heavier weight.

5,000 grams   6 kilograms

10,000 grams   12 kilograms

2,000 grams   1 kilogram

0-7424-1792-1 *Daily Warmups*

Geometry

Use a geoboard.

Copy the shape on your geoboard.
Then make another shape just like it.
Twin shapes (congruent shapes) are
the same size and shape.

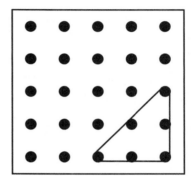

Data Analysis
and Probability

Look in your desk for pencils, crayons, and books.
Tally each one. Then make a graph to show your data.

Measurement

Measure each item using a centimeter ruler.

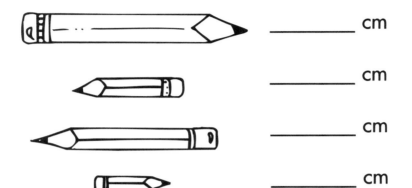

_____ cm

_____ cm

_____ cm

_____ cm

Number and Operations

Add or subtract.

485 – 213 =

286 + 613 =

719 – 613 =

328 + 283 =

0-7424-1792-1 *Daily Warmups*

Geometry

Imagine that you have a paper bag the size of this page. Put an X on the things that would not fit in the bag.

Data Analysis and Probability

Kumar has 1 green cube, 1 red cube, and 2 blue cubes in a paper bag. If he shakes the bag and takes out a cube, does he have a greater chance of getting one color more than the others? Why?

153 Measurement

When their family went to the supermarket, Erin and her brother went first to the bakery to buy fresh bread. They went to the bakery at 5:00 P.M. It took them 5 minutes to buy bread. Then they went to find vegetables for salad. This took them 20 minutes. Then they went to the café for a soda. This took them 15 minutes. Then they met their parents.

:	went to bakery
:	left bakery
:	went to café
:	met parents

154 Geometry

Use a geoboard.

Copy the shape on your geoboard.
Then make another shape like the first one.

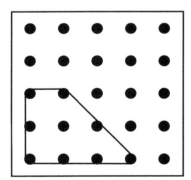

Algebra

Look at the sets of pictures shown below.
List one way the things are alike and one way
they are different.

Algebra

Fill in the missing numbers to show equal values.

_____ + 3 = 5 + 5

7 + _____ = 9 + 2

10 + 0 = _____ + 8

8 + 7 = 9 + _____

Algebra

Shade to keep the pattern going.

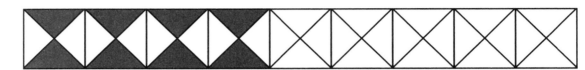

Number and Operations

Chelsea has ordered a burger, a soda, and a sundae. The burger costs $3.25. The soda costs $0.75. The sundae costs $1.25. Chelsea gives the cashier a $10.00 bill. How much change does she receive?

Measurement

Ana and 4 friends went on a camping trip. If they took along 25 liters of water, how much water was there for each person?

Problem Solving

Draw four ways to make $0.70.

Measurement

Measure each item using a centimeter ruler.

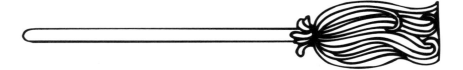

_____ cm

_____ cm

Number and Operations

Subtract.

$65 - 21 =$

$36 - 25 =$

$85 - 51 =$

$94 - 32 =$

Number and Operations

163

Write the value of each set of flats, rods, and units.

_____ hundreds _____ tens _____ ones
_____ total

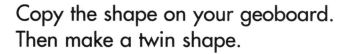

_____ hundreds _____ tens _____ ones
_____ total

Geometry

164

Use geoboard.

Copy the shape on your geoboard.
Then make a twin shape.

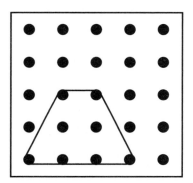

Data Analysis and Probability

Ask the students in your class: What is your favorite school subject? Tally the answers. Then make a graph to show the results.

Algebra

Look for a pattern between the IN and OUT numbers.

Use the pattern to fill in the missing numbers.

IN	5	8	11	14	17
OUT	2	5	8		

Write the rule.

Algebra

Shade to keep the pattern going.

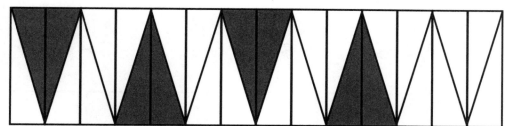

Number and Operations

There are 15 numbers on a paper. Some are less than 100, but more are greater than 100. Write the numbers.

0-7424-1792-1 *Daily Warmups*

Algebra

Color the squares shown below to make the pattern ABBCABBC.

A = red   B = orange   C = yellow

Algebra

William and his friends work in their community garden. On Monday they work 5 hours. On Tuesday they work 4 hours. On Wednesday they work 3 hours, and so on. They don't work on the weekends.

If they keep working in the same way, how many hours will they work in one week? A week is Monday through Friday. How many hours will they work in two weeks?

Number and Operations

Write the value of the coins shown below.

Measurement

Draw the hands on the clocks below to show each time.

8:30   6:00   12:30

Number and Operations

Melissa has 5 pencils. Becky has 4 pencils. Sara has 6 pencils. They want to put their pencils together. Then they want to divide them equally. Circle the number of pencils each girl will have.

Geometry

Look for cubes, rectangular prisms, and cylinders in your classroom. Tally each one that you find.

Problem Solving

Andrew and Daniel worked on their family's farm in the summer. In one day Andrew picked 84 watermelons. On the same day, Daniel picked 57 watermelons. How many more watermelons did Andrew pick than Daniel?

Number and Operations

Write three number sentences that have an answer of 15. Write one sentence with three addends.

Number and Operations

Use the clues to find the mystery number.

Clue 1 The numeral has two digits.

Clue 2 The numeral is between 1 and 50.

Clue 3 One digit of the numeral is 2.

Clue 4 The digit in the tens column is the same as the digit in the ones column.

Number and Operations

Color

the fifth fish green.
the second fish yellow.
the fourth fish orange.
the first fish blue.
the sixth fish brown.
the third fish black.
the seventh fish purple.

Data Analysis and Probability

Ask the students in your classroom: Which kind of vehicle do you think is the most popular? Tally the answers. Then make a graph to show the results.

Number and Operations

Add or subtract.

27 + 12 =

89 – 65 =

45 + 21 =

46 – 31 =

Number and Operations

Add or subtract.

46 + 22 =

65 − 31 =

57 − 12 =

17 + 52 =

Algebra

Use pattern blocks.
Look for a pattern.
A wall with 1 window takes 3 blocks to build.

If the pattern continues in the same way, how many blocks will it take to build a wall with 5 windows?

Hint: Filling in the table can help you solve the problem.

Number of windows	1	2	3	4	5
Number of blocks	3	5	7		

0-7424-1792-1 *Daily Warmups*

Algebra

Find the pattern. Then write the next numbers.

1, 3, 5, 7, _____, _____, _____, _____

Geometry

Shade each shape in the design below it.

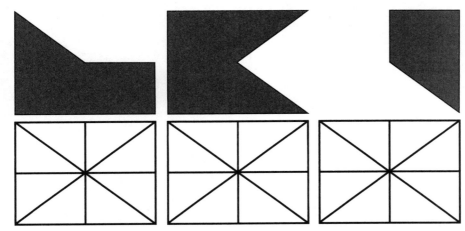

 0-7424-1792-1 *Daily Warmups*

185 Number and Operations

At the supermarket, Emily's mother buys spaghetti noodles for $1.50, spaghetti sauce for $1.25, and grated cheese for $3.00. How much does she spend in all?

186 Problem Solving

A family-sized pizza costs $24.95. Small pizzas are two for $9.99. Which would feed a family of four for the least money?

Problem Solving

Luisa has $0.25, but she has no nickels and no quarters. What coins does she have?

Number and Operations

Alida baby-sits to earn money. She also does chores for an allowance. Every Friday evening Alida gets a $5.00 allowance, and every Saturday night she makes $10.00 baby-sitting. How much money does Alida make every two weeks?

189 Algebra

Find the pattern. Then draw the figures that come next.

△, ○, □, △, ○, □, _____, _____,

_____, _____

190 Measurement

Liang's family plans to go to the movies on Saturday afternoon. The movie starts at 3 P.M., and it takes 15 minutes to walk to the theater. The movie runs for $2\frac{1}{2}$ hours. What time will Liang's family get out of the movie?

Measurement

How tall are you in centimeters?

Now find an object that is shorter than you. Measure it in centimeters. How much shorter is it than you?

Number and Operations

Write the fractions for the white portion of each figure.

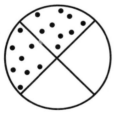 _____ white

 _____ white

Measurement

In Ms. Bailey's class, 14 liters of water were used to fill bowls that tadpoles were in. If 2 liters of water were placed in each bowl, how many bowls were filled?

Number and Operations

Add or subtract.

437 + 521 =

678 − 512 =

346 + 200 =

632 − 310 =

Measurement

Find ten items in your classroom that are between 1 and 5 inches. List them.

Number and Operations

Write the value of the coins shown below.

197 Data Analysis and Probability

Ask the students in your class: What sport do you prefer to play? Tally the answers. Then make a graph to show the results.

198 Algebra

Use cubes and a balance.

Put 3 green cubes and 5 purple cubes in one side of the balance.

Put 4 red cubes and 4 yellow cubes in the other side of the balance.

Write the equation.

Measurement

Find and measure each of the items listed.
Write the length in centimeters.

your scissors

your calculator

a book you are reading

Number and Operations

Show the different ways that you can make
$0.25 using only dimes and nickels.

201 Number and Operations

Andrew and Amanda had chores to finish before they could play with their friends. Cleaning their rooms took 15 minutes, vacuuming their rooms took 10 minutes, putting dishes into the dishwasher took 7 minutes, and taking out the trash took 3 minutes.

How long did it take them to do their chores?

202 Algebra

Use tiles.

Match each tower. Look for a pattern in the rows. Draw the next tower.

Problem Solving

Morgan is planning his Saturday schedule. He wakes up at 8:00 A.M. It takes him 30 minutes to eat breakfast and 30 minutes to get cleaned up and dressed. He has basketball practice at 10:00 A.M. Practice lasts for 1 hour and 30 minutes. What time will it be when he meets his friend Rashawn for lunch?

Measurement

Estimate the length of each object listed below. Then measure the actual length in centimeters.

a glue stick or glue bottle

Estimate _____   Measure _____

the length of an envelope

Estimate _____   Measure _____

205 Number and Operations

After the soccer game, Montell's father took him out for lunch. Montell ordered a burger for $2.00, a shake for $1.50, and fries for $0.75. How much did Montell's lunch cost?

206 Measurement

Convert each measurement from inches to feet.
12 inches = 1 foot

Christopher's father is 72 inches tall. How many feet is that?

Rana's bedroom is 60 inches in length. How many feet is that?

Algebra

Find the pattern in the numbers in the IN and OUT rows.
Use the pattern to fill in the missing numbers.

IN	4	6	8	10	12
OUT	2	3	4		

Write the rule.

Problem Solving

Draw four ways to make $0.67.

Measurement

Find ten things in your classroom that are more than 10 inches long. List them.

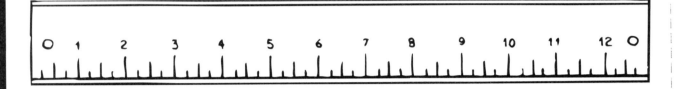

Number and Operations

Add or subtract.

867 – 352 =

298 + 312 =

499 – 126 =

328 + 283 =

Algebra

Use cubes and a balance.
Find equal values.

Put 1 blue cube and 4 green cubes on one side
of the balance.

Put 2 red cubes and 3 orange cubes on the other
side of the balance.

Write the equation.

Number and Operations

Compare the amounts by using **<**, **>**, or **=**.

3 + 7	18 − 9
14 − 7	16 − 9
8 + 5	6 + 9
17 − 8	4 + 7

Algebra

List one way the things shown are alike. Then list one way they are different.

children   and   mice

Problem Solving

Juliette and her family visit her grandmother each summer. Her grandmother lives 500 kilometers away. If Juliette's father drives 50 kilometers an hour, how long will it take to get to her grandmother's house?

Measurement

Use a ruler.

Estimate how far you think you can jump. Write your estimate in inches.

Estimate _____

Use a ruler to show where you start. Put your toes behind the ruler. Then jump.

Write how far you jumped in inches.

Measure _____

Problem Solving

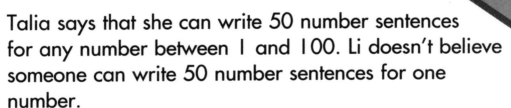

Talia says that she can write 50 number sentences for any number between 1 and 100. Li doesn't believe someone can write 50 number sentences for one number.

Show how it is possible to write 50 number sentences for one number.

Number and Operations

Write the value of the coins shown below.

Data Analysis and Probability

Use a die.

Your die has six numbers: 1, 2, 3, 4, 5, and 6. If you roll the die, your possibility of rolling a 3 is one out of six numbers.

What is the possibility you will roll a 4?

What is the possibility you will roll an odd number?

Number and Operations

Squirrels live in the trees around Kathryn's house. She often sees them carrying nuts to store for the winter. If a squirrel carries 1 nut to her nest every 2 minutes, how many nuts would she have in her nest after 1 hour?

Number and Operations

Write four number sentences that have an answer of 11.

221 Measurement

Carlos woke up at 8:30. Claudio woke up 1 hour and 15 minutes earlier. Draw the hands on the clock below to show what time Claudio woke up.

222 Data Analysis and Probability

Use a die.

Your die has six numbers: 1, 2, 3, 4, 5, and 6.

What is the possibility that you will roll a number less than 5?

What is the possibility that you will roll a 7?

Algebra

Write the names of all the things that you can find that are used for writing and drawing. Then make a chart: How are they alike? How are they different?

Number and Operations

Write four number sentences that have an answer of 14. Write one sentence with three addends.

Number and Operations

Add or subtract.

389 + 510 =

209 – 107 =

225 + 601 =

456 – 210 =

Algebra

Shade to keep the pattern going.

Number and Operations

If Lilia has 2 half-dollars, 6 dimes, 3 quarters, and 13 pennies, how much money does she have altogether?

Geometry

Think of a shape. Write three clues about it. Have a classmate guess what the shape is.

Number and Operations

Use cubes.

Take 2 blue cubes, 3 purple cubes, and 1 red cube.

_____ out of _____ cubes are blue

_____ out of _____ cubes are purple

_____ out of _____ cubes are red

Algebra

Think of an object in your classroom. Write four clues about it. Then have a classmate guess what the object is.

Measurement

Measure in inches the objects listed.

a stapler in your classroom

your favorite book

your hand from fingertips to wrist

Algebra

Find the pattern. Then fill in the missing numbers.

55, 50, 45, 40, 35, 30, _____, _____,

_____, _____

233 Number and Operations

When you add an odd and an even number together, is the answer odd or even?

Give five examples.

234 Number and Operations

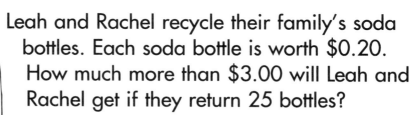

Leah and Rachel recycle their family's soda bottles. Each soda bottle is worth $0.20. How much more than $3.00 will Leah and Rachel get if they return 25 bottles?

Answer Key

Page 6
#1: Answers will vary.
#2: Students will match the shape with tangrams.

Page 7
#3: 9 P.M.; 7 hr.; 1 P.M.
#4: 29 ladybugs

Page 8
#5: 18
#6: Answers may vary; tomato; fish; banana.

Page 9
#7: 8; 9; 10
#8: $\frac{1}{4}$; $\frac{3}{8}$; $\frac{1}{2}$

Page 10
#9: 89; 42; 48; 121
#10:

Page 11
#11: Estimates will vary. All of the oranges cost $1.00.
#12: Answers may vary, but she will probably pull out a green cube, because there are more green cubes than red or yellow cubes combined.

Page 12
#13: 19; 0
#14: 7:15 A.M.

Page 13
#15: 118 lb.
#16: nectarines; apples

Page 14
#17: $0.32
#18: >; >; <

Page 15
#19: Answers will vary.
#20: 14, 16, 18

Page 16
#21: Estimates will vary. The class has raised $104.00, so they don't need to raise more money.
#22: ship; socks

Page 17
#23: Ryan, Mei, Emily, Hector, Imani
#24: 6 pieces of fudge; $0.20 change

Page 18
#25: $0.41
#26: 4; 4; 5; 10

Page 19
#27: $6.45; $3.55
#28: about 1 cm

Page 20
#29: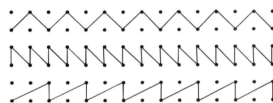

#30: $1.50

Page 21
#31: $1.00
#32: Answers may vary.

Page 22
#33: 6 hundreds, 1 ten, 6 ones, total 616; 3 hundreds, 7 tens, 2 ones, total 372
#34: 18 marbles in all, with 6 marbles for each person

Page 23
#35: 52; 54; 64; 87
#36: 37; 37; 9; 37

Page 24
#37: 16 crayons
#38: $0.45 > $0.36

Page 25
#39: Answers will vary.
#40: All the objects have wheels and transport people; answers about other objects may vary.

Page 26
#41:

#42: 399; 896; 346; 978

Page 27
#43: 2 dimes and 1 nickel or 5 nickels
#44: 331; 353; 262; 278

Page 28
#45: 12 stickers
#46: a triangle; an inverted U

Page 29
#47: 109 lb.
#48: A round bead, because there are four times as many round beads as square ones.

Page 30
#49: 3 blue counters
#50: 92 rows of plants

Page 31
#51: 117, 118, 119; 168, 169, 170; 149, 151, 152; 129, 130, 132
#52: Answers will vary. Three possible ways are two small triangles, two large triangles, or two small triangles and the parallelogram.

Page 32
#53: <; >; >
#54: the second and third groups of coins

Page 33
#55: $\frac{1}{4}$ black, $\frac{2}{4}$ black
#56: 1 quarter, 1 dime, 3 nickels, 1 penny

Page 34
#57: 9 cm; 7 cm; 10 cm
#58: =; =; =; <

Page 35
#59: 9; 8
#60:

Page 36
#61: 358; 729; 369; 198
#62:

Individual patterns will vary.

Page 37
#63: 6, 7, 8; the rule is + 3.
#64: 2 P.M.

Page 38
#65: $77.00
#66: $\frac{1}{3}$ black; $\frac{3}{4}$ black

Page 39
#67: 2
#68: 12; 8

Page 40
#69: Answers will vary.
#70: star; oval

Page 41
#71: Answers will vary.
#72: 11

Page 42
#73: 3; individual patterns will vary.
#74: 4 hr.

Page 43
#75: 40 crayons; individual pictures may vary.
#76: a triangle

Page 44
#77: Ms. Clearwater; 82 bags of produce
#78: 5; 7

Page 45
#79: Answers will vary.
#80: Answers will vary.

Page 46
#81: 8, 10, 12; the rule is + 2.
#82: 10:00 A.M.; noon

Page 47
#83: 121 books
#84: Answers will vary.

Page 48
#85: 2 units of area; 2 units of area
#86: $0.47

Page 49
#87: Results will vary, but each color has an equal chance of being drawn.
#88: $\frac{1}{2}$ black; $\frac{1}{3}$ white

Page 50
#89: Answers will vary.
#90: $0.93

Page 51
#91: 1,547 blooming daisies
#92: 710; 985; 755; 725

Page 52
#93: 9 blocks
#94: $43.00

Page 53
#95: blue, blue, green, green, blue, blue, green, green
#96: 6 pins

Page 54
#97: 25 blocks
#98: 8 sides, 8 corners

Page 55
#99: 6 in.; 4 in.
#100: 2 quarters, 5 pennies

Page 56
#101: Answers will vary.
#102: 8 units

Page 57
#103: <; <; =; <
#104: 5 + 5 = 7 + 3

Page 58
#105: 19; the pattern is +2 , +3.
#106: Answers will vary depending on the size of the paper and the size of the tiles.

Page 59
#107: 6 crayons and 10 markers or 7 crayons and 11 markers
#108:

Individual patterns will vary.

Page 60
#109: Answers will vary.
#110: 6; 8; 9; 8

Page 61
#111: K, M, O; the pattern is every other letter.
#112: brown, yellow, red, blue, orange, green, black, purple

Page 62
#113: $12.00
#114: Answers will vary, but one possible solution is a small, thick, red square; a small, thick, blue triangle; and a small, thick, yellow circle.

Page 63
#115: 5 + 5 + 5 = 8 + 2 + 5
#116: 4 pies

Page 64
#117: 5 students
#118: Answers will vary, but similarities might include that they are all mammals and have four legs; differences are that they are different sizes and live in different habitats.

Page 65
#119: outside: swings, sandbox; home: cookie jar, vacuum cleaner, chair, bathtub; classroom: stapler
#120: 7; 4

Page 66
#121: Answers will vary, but one solution is that the triangle doesn't fit because it has three sides.
#122: 331; 353; 262; 278

Page 67
#123: 24 rows of corn
#124: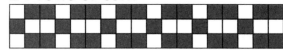

Page 68
#125: outside: slide, teeter-totter; home: bed, television; classroom: easel
#126: $\frac{5}{5}$ (1) black; $\frac{2}{3}$ black

Page 69
#127: 36 sides
#128: Answers will vary.

Page 70
#129: 40, 45, 50; the pattern is + 5. Answers on individual patterns will vary.
#130: 0 hundreds, 5 tens, 8 ones, total 58; 2 hundreds, 1 ten, 7 ones, total 217

Page 71
#131: <; >; <
#132: Answers will vary, but possible solutions are that corn and honey are a similar color but corn is solid and honey is liquid; gloves and slippers are pairs, but gloves are worn outdoors and slippers are worn indoors.

Page 72
#133: 21
#134: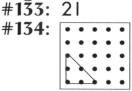

Page 73
#135: $\frac{3}{10}$ black; $\frac{3}{5}$ white
#136: Answers will vary.

Page 74
#137: Answers will vary.
#138:

Page 75
#139: 8, 9, 10; the rule is + 5.
#140: no; yes; yes

Page 76
#141: 10 lb.; 2 lb.; 14 lb.
#142: 6

Page 77
#143: Answers will vary, but examples might be a linking cube (cube), a basket or box (rectangular prism), or a mug (cylinder).
#144: 25 cm; 25 cm; 20 cm

Page 78
#145: 12 flowers
#146: 6 kg; 12 kg; 2,000 g

Page 79
#147:

#148: Answers will vary.

Page 80
#149: 6 cm; 3 cm; 5 cm; 2 cm
#150: 272; 899; 106; 611

Page 81
#151: The chicken, eagle, and hat will not fit.
#152: Kumar is more likely to draw a blue cube than a red cube or a green cude, because there are more blue cubes.

Page 82

#153: 5:00 P.M.; 5:05 P.M.; 5:25 P.M.;
5:40 P.M.

#154:

Page 83

#155: Apples and peanuts are both foods, but apples are fruits and peanuts are legumes. Bikes and balls both start with "b" or are things to play with, but bikes are ridden and balls are thrown or kicked.

#156: 7; 4; 2; 6

Page 84

#157:

#158: $4.75

Page 85

#159: about 5 liters
#160: Answers will vary.

Page 86

#161: 13 cm; 11 cm
#162: 44; 11; 34; 62

Page 87

#163: 5 hundreds, 2 tens, 2 ones, total 522; 3 hundreds, 4 tens, 8 ones, total 348

#164:

Page 88

#165: Answers will vary.
#166: 11, 14; the rule is − 3.

Page 89

#167:

#168: Answers will vary.

Page 90

#169: red, orange, orange, yellow, red, orange, orange, yellow
#170: 15 hours in the first week; 30 hours in two weeks

Page 91

#171: $0.42
#172:

Page 92

#173: 5 pencils
#174: Answers will vary.

Page 93

#175: 27 watermelons
#176: Answers will vary.

Page 94

#177: 22
#178: blue, yellow, black, orange, green, brown, purple

Page 95

#179: Answers will vary.
#180: 39; 24; 66; 15

Page 96

#181: 68; 34; 45; 69
#182: 11 blocks; in the table, 9, 11

Page 97

#183: 9, 11, 13, 15
#184:

Page 98

#185: $5.75
#186: four small pizzas for $19.98

Page 99

#187: Answers may vary; 2 dimes, 5 pennies.
#188: $30.00

Page 100
#**189**: triangle, circle, square, triangle
#**190**: 5:30 P.M.

Page 101
#**191**: Answers will vary.
#**192**: $\frac{2}{4}$ white; $\frac{6}{8}$ white

Page 102
#**193**: 7 bowls
#**194**: 958; 166; 546; 322

Page 103
#**195**: Answers will vary.
#**196**: $0.49

Page 104
#**197**: Answers will vary.
#**198**: 3 + 5 = 4 + 4

Page 105
#**199**: Answers will vary.
#**200**: 1 dime and 3 nickels; 2 dimes and 1 nickel; 5 nickels

Page 106
#**201**: 35 min.
#**202**: There will be 15 tiles in the pattern.

Page 107
#**203**: 11:30 A.M.
#**204**: Answers will vary.

Page 108
#**205**: $4.25
#**206**: 6 ft.; 5 ft.

Page 109
#**207**: 5, 6; the rule is to divide by 2.
#**208**: Answers will vary.

Page 110
#**209**: Answers will vary.
#**210**: 515; 610; 373; 611

Page 111
#**211**: 1 + 4 = 2 + 3
#**212**: >; =; <; <

Page 112
#**213**: Both are small mammals. Children walk on two legs; mice walk on four legs.
#**214**: 10 hr.

Page 113
#**215**: Answers will vary.
#**216**: Some hints: What two numbers equal the number? Use more than two numbers. Add a number to the chosen number. Then use the new, larger number in a subtraction problem.

Page 114
#**217**: $0.87
#**218**: 1 out of 6 numbers; 3 out of 6 numbers

Page 115
#**219**: 30 nuts
#**220**: Answers will vary.

Page 116
#**221**: 7:15
#**222**: 4 out 6; 0 out of 6

Page 117
#**223**: Answers will vary.
#**224**: Answers will vary.

Page 118
#**225**: 899; 102; 826; 246
#**226**:

Page 119
#**227**: $2.48
#**228**: Answers will vary.

Page 120
#**229**: 2 out 6 blue; 3 out of 6 purple; 1 out of 6 red
#**230**: Answers will vary.

Page 121
#**231**: Answers will vary.
#**232**: 25, 20, 15, 10

Page 122
#**233**: odd; examples will vary.
#**234**: $2.00 more